O9-BUC-425

PRAISE FOR *HARD TIMES REQUIRE FURIOUS DANCING*

"Since Walker's *The Color Purple* appeared in 1982, she has remained one of America's best-loved writers for the passion and purpose of her work. Her poetry, like her prose, is direct and sonorous. In this collection, she writes of loss and disappointment, and the strength that rises from meeting them unflinchingly."

— Patricia Monaghan, *Booklist*

"These poems are so beautiful, so full of truth and light, that it is possible to forget how absolutely useful they are. And how necessary. Alice Walker has given us a year of poems that speak to us like wise old friends, reminding us to embrace our freedom; encouraging us to celebrate our love; and demanding that in the face of things known, and things unknowable, we grab another human being by the hand and *dance* as often, and as furiously, as we possibly can!"

— Pearl Cleage, author of *We Speak Your Names*

"The intimacy and grace of her words are a call to love more deeply, no matter what we have endured. Her poems are medicine for the soul."

— from the foreword by Shiloh McCloud

HARD TIMES
REQUIRE FURIOUS
DANCING

OTHER BOOKS BY ALICE WALKER

NOVELS

*By the Light
of My Father's Smile*

Meridian

*Now Is the Time
to Open Your Heart*

Possessing the Secret of Joy

The Color Purple

The Temple of My Familiar

*The Third Life
of Grange Copeland*

SHORT STORIES

*In Love & Trouble:
Stories of Black Women*

*You Can't Keep
a Good Woman Down*

*The Way Forward
Is with a Broken Heart*

POETRY

*Absolute Trust in the Goodness
of the Earth*

*A Poem Traveled
Down My Arm*

*Good Night Willie Lee,
I'll See You in the Morning*

*Her Blue Body
Everything We Know*

*Horses Make a Landscape Look
More Beautiful*

Once

Revolutionary Petunias

NONFICTION

*Anything We Love
Can Be Saved*

*In Search of Our Mothers'
Gardens: Womanist Prose*

Living by the Word

*Overcoming Speechlessness:
A Poet Encounters the Horror. . . .*

*Sent by Earth: A Message by the
Grandmother Spirit. . . .*

*The Same River Twice:
Honoring the Difficult*

*We Are the Ones
We Have Been Waiting For*

CHILDREN'S BOOKS

Finding the Green Stone

*Langston Hughes,
American Poet*

*There Is a Flower at the Tip of
My Nose Smelling Me*

To Hell with Dying

Why War Is Never a Good Idea

COAUTHORED BOOKS

Warrior Marks
(with Pratibha Parmar)

INTERVIEWS

*The World Has Changed:
Conversations with Alice Walker*

HARD TIMES REQUIRE FURIOUS DANCING

NEW POEMS BY
ALICE WALKER

Foreword and illustrations by SHILOH McCLOUD

A PALM OF HER HAND PROJECT

New World Library
Novato, California

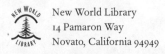 New World Library
14 Pamaron Way
Novato, California 94949

Copyright © 2010 by Alice Walker

All rights reserved. This book may not be reproduced in whole or in part, stored in a retrieval system, or transmitted in any form or by any means — electronic, mechanical, or other — without written permission from the publisher, except by a reviewer, who may quote brief passages in a review.

Illustrations and cover design by Shiloh McCloud with Michelle Noe
www.shilohsophia.com

 A Palm of Her Hand Project
www.palmofherhand.com

Text design by Tona Pearce Myers

Library of Congress Cataloging-in-Publication Data
Walker, Alice, date.
Hard times require furious dancing : new poems / by Alice Walker ; foreword and illustrations by Shiloh McCloud.
   p.   cm.
"A Palm of Her Hand project."
ISBN 978-1-57731-930-6 (hardcover : alk. paper)
I. Title.
PS3573.A425H37 2010
811'.54—dc22   2010029972

First paperback printing, September 2013
Originally published in hardcover in 2010
ISBN 978-1-60868-188-4
Printed in the USA on 100% postconsumer-waste recycled paper

 New World Library is proud to be a Gold Certified Environmentally Responsible Publisher. Publisher certification awarded by Green Press Initiative. www.greenpressinitiative.org

10 9 8 7 6 5 4 3

To
Sarah Lawrence College
&
Mexico:
place
&
land
of
my
rebirth.

And
to my home buddies:
Surprise,
Garrett Kaleo
&
Miles

Great Presence
Everywhere
I thank you
for all your blessings.
I
am yours;
everything
I know I learn from you.

CONTENTS

*H*ard Times Require Furious Dancing was conceived over the course of a year. Alice Walker's journey, revealed in this writing, includes the death of loved ones and the birth of new ideas, the sorrow of rejection and the deliciousness of love, travel to other parts of the world and the sweetness of home, the challenges of our world and its blessings, familial abandonment and what it means to belong to the greater world family.

Once again we are witness to the self-confidence that so profoundly distinguishes Alice's work — her ability to take that which is heart-wrenchingly sad, to share the guts of that sadness, and then, through a tapestry of richly colored words, to weave a resolution that leaves the poem with a way to "be with" that sorrow instead of becoming drowned in it. She does not leave the poem or the reader in distress but soothes the aching heart with true poetry:

This we know:
We were
not meant
to suffer
so much
& to learn
nothing.

Along with the poet, we are drawn into kinds of suf-
fering for which we may have no words; Alice gives
them to us as offerings. She writes to the woman who
was stoned to death: "You will never/know/how/
much/I loved/you." She writes to Burmese opposi-
tion activist Aung San Suu Kyi: "Loving humans/
makes us/want/to invite/ourselves to tea/with ran-
cid/dictators." Dictators who may be thinking, as we
dream, of how to murder us with their teacups.

   We are privileged to accompany this remarkable
poet on her journey in the dawn of her sixty-fifth year.
We taste the fruits of her days, share in the ripe lan-
guage of acceptance — "I will keep/broken/things"
— and the sting of wisdom as she tells us, "There is
no/graceful/way/to/carry/hatred." We hear what
she says to the grandson she has never met:

nothing
will
ultimately separate
us:

not
space
not
time
not unanticipated
turbulence
&
discord.

The intimacy and grace of her words are a call to love more deeply, no matter what we have endured. Her poems are medicine for the soul.

On reading her work, we find the courage to reach into our own suffering and to draw out the beauty there. Alice Walker's willingness to share her life at the depths calls us to look at our own lives and relationships and to consider: How are we living? What is our response to those who hate us? How are we to respond to the cruelty of the world? Alice encourages those around her, and her readers, to find peace amid the chaos, to go deeper into ourselves where "the body & the soul / come back / together."

The title chosen for this book, *Hard Times Require Furious Dancing*, perfectly introduces the poetry in these pages. Those words were written in an invitation to a celebration Alice hosted, calling us to come and dance through whatever challenged us. Palm of Her Hand designed that invitation, and from there, the first card with that quotation was born.

One year ago Palm of Her Hand helped launch Alice Walker's website and blog. New poems were called for. Conceived out of Alice's experiences in Northern California, Mexico, Egypt, Palestine, and Myanmar, these poems were birthed organically, through the poet's heart expressing itself onto particles of stardust, and were first published on the people's medium, the web.

Alice is a witness, someone who can show up on the front lines and stand for justice and then go home to peace and simplicity. She can travel to war-ravaged countries and come back with new friends, new families, new directions and responsibilities and poems. She has chosen to be happy, while still remaining present to the world. And that is her call to us.

— Shiloh McCloud

PREFACE

Learning to Dance

I am the youngest of eight siblings. Five of us have died. I share losses, health concerns, and other challenges common to the human condition, especially in these times of war, poverty, environmental devastation, and greed that are quite beyond the most creative imagination. Sometimes it all feels a bit too much to bear. Once a person of periodic deep depressions, a sign of mental suffering in my family that affected each sibling differently, I have matured into someone I never dreamed I would become: an unbridled optimist who sees the glass as always full of something. It may be half full of water, precious in itself, but in the other half there's a rainbow that could exist only in the vacant space.

I have learned to dance.

It isn't that I didn't know how to dance before; everyone in my community knew how to dance, even those with several left feet. I just didn't know how basic it is for maintaining balance. That Africans are always dancing (in their ceremonies and rituals) shows an awareness of this. It struck me one day, while dancing, that the marvelous moves African Americans are famous for on the dance floor came about because the dancers, especially in the old days, were contorting away various knots of stress. Some of the lower-back movements handed down to us that have seemed merely sensual were no doubt created after a day's work bending over a plow or hoe on a slave driver's plantation.

Wishing to honor the role of dance in the healing of families, communities, and nations, I hired a local hall and a local band and invited friends and family from near and far to come together, on Thanksgiving, to dance our sorrows away, or at least to integrate them more smoothly into our daily existence. The next generation of my family, mourning the recent death of a mother, my sister-in-law, created a spirited line dance that assured me that, though we have all encountered our share of grief and troubles, we can still hold the line of beauty, form, and beat — no small accomplishment in a world as challenging as this one.

Hard times require furious dancing. Each of us is the proof.

HARD TIMES
REQUIRE FURIOUS
DANCING

YES, I KNOW

Yes, I know I am not
a farmer
and that you
are
not
a gypsy
or a king:
Have you ever
heard
of
poetic license?
It is when
for instance
the poet
writes
buffaloes
instead
of *buffalo*
because
their
numbers
are now
so
thin

&
she
does
not
want
the remaining
tiny
herds
to feel
lonely.

I claim
farming ancestry:
Generations
going back
sometimes
farther
than
I wish
to look:
All those Africans
& their
yam & cassava fields
the Indians &
their corn
&
beans
the English

& their
collard plants
the Scots
their
what?
crabgrass?
maybe oats!
the Irish
their potatoes
the Elves
their
herbs.

All killing themselves
now
by the thousands
farmers
killing themselves
by
their own
calloused
hands;
not just
in India,
where suicide
among
farmers
is

a leading cause
of
death
but in
America
too
they are doing
it.

How can this be?
And how can
we
bear
the
loss?

So I claim
them
in
myself:
I
am
that.

I too
run after
the Earth
as it disappears

beneath
my feet;

I too
mourn
machines moving
over her face
without
empathy
or
love
of
her.

Even so,
you are
quite right:
I am not
a "farmer"
as most
would think
of
it:
Tilling my tiny
plots
of corn
&
beans;

collards
&
squash;
strawberries:
Leaning more
&
more
on the strength
& youth
of
others
as time
moves on.

No, I was born to grow,
alongside my garden of plants,
poems
like
this one:

I was born to grow,
alongside my garden of plants,
poems like this one

You confide
in me
that
you
are lonely,

that romance
juicy
&
red
never stays
long
at
your
house.
But when
I visit
you
what
do I
find?

You do not
own
a sofa!

Without
a sofa
preferably
burgundy
or maroon
you cannot
expect
to
have romance
come
&
stay
in your
house.

A sofa is
essential
to all
that
lures
romance
to
your boudoir;

I cannot
believe
you are
so old
&

do not
know
this.

Well, lucky
for you
I am older!

Trying to have
romance
sit down,
visit
&
decide to
stay
with
you
when you have
no sofa
on
which
to sit
is like
using one
hand
in the
vast

ocean
to
catch
a
large fish.

YOU'D BE SURPRISED

You'd be surprised
to find
how cleansing
it feels
to depose
a
dictator:
There she is
anticipating your
every wish
seeking to orchestrate
your every
desire.
Get rid of her!
Life is too broad
a country
to tolerate
such foolishness
in your
own
small
yard.

VASILISA

My sisters
abandoned me.
I might have
died
from their
calculated
indifference
& neglect.
Still
I ran after
them
like a beggar
holding
out
my trust.

SOMETIMES

Sometimes
who knows how?
the body & the soul
come back
together
again
the hand
holding the pen
writes
not advertising
but
heart.

Sometimes
who knows how?
the body & the soul
come back together
again

EASY

When I understood
you were
a tiger
learning to love
& not
devour
a monkey
I could rest
easy
under
your paws.

COMPATIBLE

We are not
compatible
said the
tiger
to
the bear.
The tiger
was spitting
out blackberry
seeds
barely disguising
his
disgust.
The bear
was feeling
foolish
a leaping
antelope
between
his teeth.

THE ANSWER IS YES

You must
run around like a
crazy person
or
walk
sedately
honoring
the
dead.

MY TEACHER

Marley Mu came into my life when life was
    dragging
and while teaching her how to pee in the right
    place,
eat without too much slobber
kiss me without stopping up my nose
she made me see that life is always
wonderful
it is only us
who
get off track
&
cannot see
the magic.

We were together
thirteen long years,
good years,
& she was my
teacher.

All her life
I knew where she was
every night
except two.

There were many who loved her.
And even one night when she
was lost
her sweet spirit sent her rescuers
to find me.

I will miss her, the Marley Mu
who came to live
with me
& yet
one other thing
she taught
is that
there is only one
Mu
& so
I learned
that she is the sweet
black Lab
— on the beach
in the street —
still
coming
lovingly
to greet
me
everywhere.

Alice Walker Mu — June 13, 2008

THIS ROOM

This room
is very powerful:
Buddha, golden,
holding down one side;
the primordial
Great Mother, black,
offering her
bead
of mitochondria
holding down
the other.
My meditation
chairs
are made of wicker
a miracle
crafted by
human hands.
Human being
may I not
forget you
in all
this talk
of God.

STILL

I have found
powerful
love
among
my sisters
I have
shredded
every
veil
and still
believe
in them.

LOST

My daughter
is lost
to me
but I am not
lost:
She says
freedom
to her
means
having a loving
mother;
which
as Mu* is my witness,
I have been
&
am.

However:

Liberation
is in
the heart

---

* *Mu*, the Buddha's word for Earth.

of
the tethered
as Harriet**
teaches us.
I bow
to
this history
&
our difference.

Freedom
to me
means
love itself
may not
be
chained
&
that
I
at the very least

may
own
myself.

** Harriet Tubman, whose free heart prevented her from
being a slave.

Freedom

to me

means

love itself

may not

be

chained

IN US

In us
the old dark
Indians
reappear

who were
not
wrong

though
chopped
in half
for living
on their
sacred
lands.

In us
the old
dark
Indians
reappear
silent
disclosing

our
massacres
by our
lack
of
trust

silent
unmoved
by
word or
deed

straight
of
back
&
silent
above all
in our
wooden
chairs.

We have to live
differently

or we
will die
in the same

old ways.

Therefore
I call on all Grand Mothers
everywhere
on the planet
to rise
and take your place
in the leadership
of the world

Come out
of the kitchen
out of the
fields
out of the
beauty parlors

out of the
television

Step forward
& assume
the role
for which
you were
created:
To lead humanity
to health, happiness
& sanity.

I call on
all the
Grand Mothers
of Earth
& every person
who possesses
the Grand Mother
spirit
of respect for
life
&
protection of
the young
to rise
& lead.

The life of
our species
depends
on it.

& I call on all men
of Earth
to gracefully
and
gratefully

stand aside
& let them
(let us)
do so.

I call on
all the
Grand Mothers
of Earth
& every person
who possesses
the Grand Mother
spirit

ONE EARTH

One Earth
One People
One Love

One Earth
One People
One Love

One Earth
One People
One Love

THE TASTE OF GRUDGE

The soul knows pain but is never diminished, injured,
or destroyed. Thank you, Clarissa, for teaching this.

I.

How many
times
life
has
seemed
too steep
a
hill
to
climb
how
many times
the hill
has disappeared
like
mist.

I am carried
in arms
that planned
adventure
for
my life

I sit nowhere
I am
told
to
stand.

II.

You
will
concern
me
in
my dreams
&
in my
hour
of
death:

I love you
in & out
of
all
assignments.

Obviously
we
had
work

to
do.

III.

Do not fight
the despair
of
harming
me.
To my
kindness
you
have
been
rude
&
more.
Something
in life
evens
every
score
&
I am left
to
say
even
if I disappear

be
safe.

IV.

Let the
joyful
heart
that
knows
the
dance
return!
Sorrow has
banished
it,
grief
has
stilled
my feet.
But there
remains
internal
movement
toward
life's
margin
where
all

begins
again
in
solemn
beat.

V.

Who can
completely
stop
a gift?

My love
will flow
around
your
rocks
break
your
dam
& live
in
all
the
trampled
plants
of
your

fouled
wilderness.

It is a bright
spring
glowing
rippling
overflowing
in
the
shade.

I do not
regret
that
I am
imperfect.

In each crack
there is
an orchid
growing

& chocolate
serves
me
when

I
slip
from
grace.

I do not
relish
perfection
or sainthood.

Flying
through
this
existence
as
myself
I honor
all
the
fierce
edges
I have
made
for
myself
&
the conundrums
I have

made
for
you.

VI.

There is
no God
but
love
which
is
what
I
have
become.

Just a
part
a
tiny
part
of
it

beyond
anger
beyond
blame

but
not
beyond
the
peace
still
possible
to
all
in this
world.

VII.

I do not
mourn
that is not
the feeling
I have
but rather
I feel
the
cool
darkness
inside
me
steady
as a
slowly

flowing
stream.

It glimmers
& glows
but
little
yet
lights my way.

VIII.

You have hit
a wall
that
was
my
open heart.

Protection
(not closure)
has
sprung up
like
those
weeds
in
Mexico
we eat

in
salads.

It
just grows
there
sent
by
angels
the same ones
ageless
who are
always
looking out
for me.

I may die
tonight
perhaps you
are killing
me.
I do not
blame you
for anything.
You were
part of
the work
I was given
on

this
trip.
You did
your
part.
I did
mine.

IX.

The journey
of death
the journey
to death
I do not
fear.
When you smell
a rose
or see one
or
see a
doe
or jackrabbit,
a leaf,
a star
there
I
will be.
Sooner
or later

& you
will see: No anger
followed me.
No injury.
No blame.

X.

Save yourself!
It can be done.
Even if the mind
is
shambled
sit still
place
your
back
against
a tree
like Buddha
& steady
it.
Silence it.
It wants
to go on
possessing
controlling
raging
dictating
lying.

Save yourself!
It can be done.
Even if the mind
is
shambled
sit still
place
your
back
against
a tree

But life's
too short!

You'll wake up
in the
night
one day
&
it will all
— this life —
be over!

What a waste
is any kind
of
grudge.

The taste
of
grudge
destroys
completely
the
taste
of
cherries.

Wake up!
before it is

too late:
Rejoice
to have
the
noble
dwelling
of
your body
with all
its
teeth!

XI.

Let the wind
talk
to you
on the moor,
like
Jane Eyre
& your
sister's
heroes
in
books
that
threw
a lifeline
across

abyss after
abyss
of craziness.

XII.

We did what
we could
with what
was
forced
on us.

No regrets.
No blame.
The taste
of figs
cherries
peaches
mangoes
orange peel
scent

with blind
luck
& many
tribulations
we made it

to
this
world!

XIII.

Rise! Rising
as Maya
reminds us
is our
way
with
devastation.
There is
no
god
but
love
&
so
rising is
inherent
in
our
heartbeat
as we
move
carried or

knocked
about
by life.

This we know:
We were
not meant
to suffer
so much
& to learn
nothing.

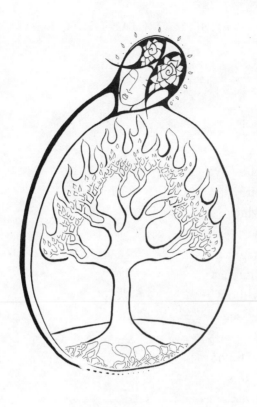

There is

no

god

but

love

LOVE IS THAT GIANT BAG

Love
is that giant
bag
of everything
into
which
we
might
disappear
without
a trace
&
be found
again:
Even
the parent
you
thought
was
lost.

Father,
gone to spirit
before

you reached
my
age,
I am
your
dream
of
me
&
more
&
I will
carry
us,
plucked
from
love's
abyss.

WATCHING YOU HOLD YOUR HATRED

Watching you
hold
your
hatred
for such a long time
I wonder:
Isn't it
slippery?
Might you
not
someday
drop it
on
yourself?

I wonder:
Where does it sleep
if ever?

And where
do
you deposit
it
while you

feed
your
children
or

sit
in the
lap
of
the one
who
cherishes
you?

There is no
graceful
way
to
carry
hatred.

While
hidden
it is
everywhere.

I WILL KEEP BROKEN THINGS

I will keep
broken
things:
The big clay
pot
with raised
iguanas
chasing
their
tails;
two
of their
wise
heads
sheared
off;

I will keep
broken
things:
The old
slave
market
basket

brought
to my
door
by Mississippi
a jagged
hole
gouged
in its sturdy
dark
oak
side.

I will keep
broken
things:
The memory
of
those
long
delicious
night
swims
with
you;

I will keep
broken
things:

In my house
there
remains
an
honored
shelf
on which
I will
keep
broken
things.

Their beauty
is
they
need
not
ever
be
"fixed."

I will keep
your
wild
free
laughter
though
it is now

missing
its
reassuring
and

graceful
hinge.

I will keep
broken
things:

*Thank you
so much!*

I will keep
broken
things.
I will keep
you:

pilgrim
of
sorrow.

I will keep
myself.

LA VACA*

For Marco

Look
into
her eyes
and know:
She does not think
of
herself
as
steak.

---

* *La Vaca*, "the cow" in Spanish.

MONKEYS ARE CURIOUS

We want
to know.

Monkeys are curious.
We ask
ourselves:
Will the tiger
bite
will the snake
choke
will the dragon
charm
will the elephant
trample us?

Will the pig entertain?

We want
to know
these
things.

I KNOW MY DUTY TO LIFE

I know
my duty
to life,

I was not
born
tomorrow;

how could
I know
how
hard
it
will be?

Our children
cooked
by
an
indifferent
sun

once a Goddess;
now

through
negligence
& scanty praise
simply
fire.

I know
my duty
to life,

to stop
wars
especially
those
I cause
within
myself.

Who knew?
Fights
with ourselves
each
other
&
her
led
to the
encirclement

of
the globe
in
ice
& all our
beloved
cousins
furry
&
nonfurry
stuck
in
it
forever?

I know
my duty
to life:

I am grateful to have
even a glimpse
of it!

Life
gives me
this hammock
a close-up
view

of hand-plastered
walls
& blue
forget-me-nots
that bloom
within
eyes'
reach.

Yes
it is life
that has given
me
this swinging
white
hammock
made of
string
by
humble
hands
that
still
pray;
this hammock
sold
for a dollar
on a beach

littered
shamefully
but
still
beautiful
&
pure.

I see
that I,
though
not
born
tomorrow,
am permitted —
swinging
suspended
in time —
to see it
from
here.

I know my duty to life,

to stop wars
especially
those I cause
within
myself.

Word has reached me
that you are dying
you, who hid
in the closet
the morning
I was born
to witness
my birth
— investigative Scorpio —
and did not believe in cabbage
or stork.

I am far away
not only in distance
from your bed
but
in emotion.

Calling hospice
I hear
your quite loud
moans
of resistance:
You do not want to go
& even dying

you will not pretend
otherwise.

Oprah you will miss
you have said, your
most
beloved,
& all your friends
from television
who
kept
you
company:
befriending you
through pain
&
drama
over
so many
searing
&
tumultuous
years.

I, once so close
have drifted.

Yesterday
my friends and I chanted

for an hour
an ancient mantra
for sending
loved ones on their way
with kindness
&
no fear.

We lit candles
& incense
&
in my chanting
vision
I saw you
seating yourself
(dressed in black: centered
and calm)
in a small boat
ochre colored
both
boat
&
sail.

Let go, let go
into the soothing river
channel
I said to you

& you
looked
as though
you were considering
it.

Hearing your voice
over thousands
of miles
no words
only
sounds of protest
of struggle
of fighting —
it is so
you.
So much
your
essence
I hear in
the argument
you make.

Praying, later,
I sent word
to you that both our parents
are waiting
— all, whatever it was

that rankled —
is now
& forevermore
forgiven:
Grandpa & Grandma
are
waiting too.

How they loved & what is more, understood, you.
I wonder if or why
you fear them?

As for me,
I am
spending the morning
thinking of you
feeling with you
and wishing
you
ease
&
peace.

Sweeping up the petals
of flowers
that surround
my door
I see your face

all our faces
swept away
by life's good
broom
whenever
&
wherever
we fall.

Let go. *Off into the river*
channel. Let go.
All is well.
The love we shared as children
is not lost, though we have been.

Let go.
Let go.
Let go.

I pray
for you
to love
the precious
body
this
lifetime
has
given
you
as I love it.

In youth
every speeding
motorcycle
beckoned
to turn
itself
over
on
you:

Knives
held

by
goons
found
their way
into
your
blameless
flesh:

Somehow
you broke
both
your shoulders
&
many
helpful
bones
in legs
&
feet.

I can hardly
bear
to touch
the scarred
ridges
under the
sweet

hair
on
your
so
frequently
battered
head;
you
have
crashed
into
life
repeatedly,
thinking
perhaps
you
are
a
bull.

O
Holy One
so
filled
with
compassion
for even
the tiniest

fly
why must
it be
that
dismissing
endless roses
saluting
us
in this world
if there
is
anywhere
a
thorn
you
will
walk
into
it?

I will not deny
my lips
their smile
I will not deny
my heart
its sorrow
I will not deny
my eyes
their tears
I will not deny
my hair
the wildness
of my age

It is
profound
selfishness

I will deny
me nothing
of myself.

YOU WILL NEVER KNOW

You will never
know
how
much
I loved
you
as
I watched
them
stone
you
in the film.

Cowards,
they covered
up
your body
& your
face
so they
would not
have
to notice
you.

There is a stone
the perfect
size
to crush
your skull
another
just right
to bash
the delicate
bridge
of
your nose:
Still another,
needle edged
with
which
to gash
open
or
bruise shut
your
eyes.

Your pink
shroud
that
you
must

wear
every day
of
your
life
has
a tiny
window:
Did you
bother
to look
out of it
to
see?

Your neighbors
and
their boys
would have
been there:

Children
have to learn.

Perhaps your own
sons
were encouraged
to throw

the first
stone.

I don't speak
of Jesus
as much
as some do —
though
I
miss
him
just
as
much:

Still, how right
he was —
honoring
the feminine
in woman
the Earth
&
himself —
to try
to put
a stop
to this.

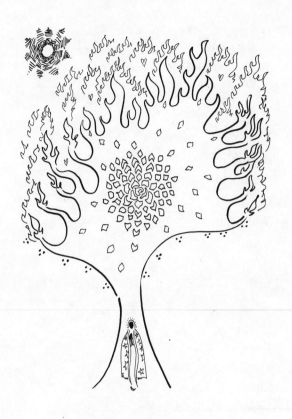

Still, how right
he was —
honoring the feminine
in woman
the Earth
&
himself

HERE

To my sixteen-year-old Beamer

Here
I
inhabit
the world
of
Wabi-sabi:

Anything
new
in
this
place
aged
long
ago.

There is
nothing
without
nicks
&
dents
scratches
&
rips;

both
night
gown
&
table
cloth
have
holes.

This is not
because
once
upon
a
time
I was
poor:

Poor,
we
would
have
hated
this.

It is
that
now
I imitate

what
Leonard*
calls
the
real
masterpiece:

Some
part
of which
is
always
tearing
dissolving
rotting
being
blown
away
by
wind
or eaten
up
by
bugs.
The
Wabi-sabi

---

* Poet Leonard Cohen.

of
Earth
makes
us
want
to let
our stairs
&
our
chairs
creak;

to let
our
teenagers —
tattered
&
pierced —
be
our
cars.

Kept from
your birth
still I realize
we
will someday
meet.

Hello, you might
begin the conversation.
Are you
my grandmother?
And I,
being your
cheeky monkey twin,
may reply:
Maybe.

Or I might begin:
Yo, cute boy,
are you
my grandchild?
& you,
cautious Capricorn,
might reply:
It's possible.

You will see
living as you do
in the Aquarian
Age
when it is
at last
possible
for mere
thought
to quickly
transform
the world —
nothing
will
ultimately separate
us:
not
space
not
time
not unanticipated
turbulence
&
discord.

Life
keeps us apart
now
for a reason

only it
knows:
Understanding
this
we have only
to endure
a separation
that
instantly
disappears
whenever you
or I
smell
a
flower.

Perhaps
like all gods
in whom
we must
have trust
Life,
Grandmother's
god
of choice,
is simply
testing
us.

You will see
living as you do
in the Aquarian Age
when it is possible for mere thought
to quickly transform the world —
nothing will ultimately separate us

The world has changed:
Wake up & smell
the possibility.
The world
has changed:
It did not
change
without
your prayers
without
your faith
without
your determination
to
believe
in liberation
&
kindness;
without
your
dancing
through the years
that had
no
beat.

The world has changed:
It did not
change
without
your
numbers
your
fierce
love
of self
&
cosmos
it did not
change
without

your
strength.

The world has
changed:
Wake up!
Give yourself
the gift
of a new
day.

The world has changed:
This does not mean

you were never
hurt.

The world
has changed:
Rise!
Yes
&
shine!
Resist the siren
call
of
disbelief.

The world has changed:
Don't let
yourself
remain
asleep
to
it.

Wake up & smell
the possibility.

SOME LOVERS

Some lovers are born
with a sweet talk deficiency.

Have you noticed?
Some lovers
can only say honey
if they're
reading
it
off a jar.

Sweetheart
& sugar
make them
think
of
cow's brains.

When they
hear the word
heart
it makes
them think
of Mother

therefore
of bread.
And
of her teaching
about
how to
dress up
less tasty
parts of
a carcass:
like
spleen.

Sugar
they've
lately
learned
is
poison
so —
no need
to go
there.

I happen
to like
a lover
who

can
be redundant
with
the sweetness
somebody
who
can really
pour
it on.

Sweetheart, sweet'ums,
sugar darling, honey
pie
what's for
dinner
or
where
was the last place
you saw
my tie?

This is a joke
of course
the last
time
I saw
the tie
of wool
or cotton

this
one
might lose,
a sheep
or a plant
was
wearing
it.

How cruel
a lack
is
this deficiency
in
sweet talk!

You're
my little sugar
dumpling
is so
much
easier
on the
snuggling
than
having
that
woman
with

the master's
degree
visibly
stop
herself
from
calling
you
madam.

My name
is not
my name
you want
to shout:
It is
a label
for those
who will
never
understand
content.

So what if all
he knows
(for your sake)
is how
to wash
the dishes

leaving
your kitchen
spotless
& your
floor
with
a shine.

So what
if the thing
she does
best
truth be told
is
crochet edges
onto old
flour
sacks
she found
in
a thrift
shop
that
just
closed.

There he is
there she is
listening

to the Temptations
& Martha and the Vandellas
& moaning

right
along.

Baby darling
sugar sweetness
honey peaches
agave princess
stevia muffin
what's wrong
with my precious
mango, apricot, watermelon, papaya
chutney
bliss
this morning?

Come to Mama
come to Papa
let's
dance
those old sugar
too much sweetness!
blues
away.

TOLD

My teacher
was told
by
her teacher —
who loved
her:

You cannot
shoot guns
you cannot
drop bombs
your fists
are forbidden
to you
as are
mean and
hurtful
words
no matter
how
carefully
chosen.

You have one
weapon

&
one weapon
only:

Use it.

It is
your
ability
to
teach.

You have one weapon
& one weapon only:

Use it.

It is your ability to teach.

TO A RELATIVE

This is all
your cruelty
to me
really
means:

We are
from different
stars.

SIXTY-FIVE!

Sixty-five!
who can
believe it.

Why not
fifty-six
or even
thirty-five?

Though it is true
some things are
smaller
or larger

shorter
or longer

tighter
or looser

less
or far
more
or less glorious.

COMMITMENT

Words for our union

Out of the fullness
of a grateful
heart
and in absolute
awe
of the power
of love
I have experienced
with
Marley (age thirteen)
and Surprise
(maybe five)
I have
with their
consent
I am sure
called
this ceremony
of commitment
of sacred
and
everlasting
union.

It is my
intention
to be
the protector,
counselor,
and guardian,
their beloved
& devoted
human,
all the
rest
of their
days;
to live
and love
with them
freely,
in the
resonant
bliss
we
have
created
so
splendidly
together.

I call
on all

our friends
two-legged
& four-legged
& maybe
winged
to witness
this
intention
& to bear
the word
to all
who may
inquire
should
I be
absent
that
these beings
are to receive
priority
in care,
in love,
in shelter
and
all things
that make
them
happy. Forever.

My love
for them
is
boundless
as theirs
for me
is
palpable.

Words cannot
express
this place
of
understanding.

I bow
to them
for their
teaching
of it
to me.

Three deep bows.

Blessed be!

WE PAY A VISIT TO THOSE
WHO PLAY AT BEING DEAD

For Rudolph, Beverly, Henri, Alice, Garrett, Angel,
Pratibha, Kiietti, Arbie

My mother
for instance
whose
cheekbones
greet me
from
a
recent
photograph
of myself.

My father:
Those eyes
in the
mirror
I would
recognize
anywhere.

My brother's
tree,
which he planted
years
before

he
was
planted
himself,
is awash
in light
robustly
proclaiming
his
vivid
if
persistently
mysterious
presence.

My grandparents
Henry
& Rachel
whose voices
are
perpetually
murmuring
sweet nothings
in my
heart.

Look!
I say to all
of them:

the cousins
&
the
outside
children
too —
I have
brought
friends!

We sit
content
&
munch
our
veggie salad
& forbidden
potato
chips
sitting
serene
among
your graves.

You are silent.

A granddaughter,
my niece,

who cares
that your
graves
are kept
clean
as she
has always
known
them,
lowers
her
shapely
form
to rest
on an army veteran's
tombstone.

So many
of you —
I had not noticed
this before —
went off
to fight
strangers!

Returning
wounded
dead

or
strangers
yourselves.

You are quiet, too, as we sit
munching
our lunch.

But are
you really
dead?

Are you not
perhaps
the reason
I have no
enthusiasm
patience
or admiration
for war?

You,
the
poor
dispossessed
cannon
fodder

safer behind
the mule
you
left
than
behind
any
gun?

My friend
Pratibha (her name means "genius" in her
original language,
which is Hindi)
brown
Indian
British
with
an accent
that
would
have
made
you laugh
(as your own Southern country accent
amused many)
films
us all

sitting
talking
eating
laughing
being with
you,

as you
play dead.

Later in
the van
leaving
your place
of enchanted
rest
we marvel
at whom
life
has put into
our vehicle.

Old friends
by now
really
because
of you.

There is
no other
explanation
though
you
may
continue
your little
afterlife game
of
playing dead.

SOMETIMES OUR DISAPPOINTMENT

For you, for your sorrow

Sometimes
our disappointment
possesses
a purity:
Sometimes
we are merely
blind.

My friend —
who could be
me
or any one
of us —
tells me,
tears
streaming
through
her voice:

I thought he was a cupcake
& instead he is
a biscuit.

My friend
is known

for her
good cooking
as we might be
too.
Still
for years
those
around her
witnessed
the unhoneyed
bitterness
kneaded
into
the flour
of this biscuit;
the greased
lightning
rage
and
unseasoned
scorn
pounded
into
the
dough.

Until,
finally,
all sweetness

beaten away,
this biscuit,
much like biscuits
you and I have known
was baked
in
nobody's
oven
but
her own.

YOU CAME

You came
into
my life
to graze

because
you
were
starving.

Having
gorged
until
you
are full

you are
displeased
by my
hunger.

It takes
so little
to make
me happy:
An hour
of planting
cucumbers
squash
tomatoes
is
an
hour
filled
with
gold.

We have all lost
much
of what
we thought
was
safely
tucked away:
To

a dragon
called
stock market
called
Wall Street
called
the economy
called
despair
&
wrong choices
around
the globe.

Still,
to be rich
in this way:
Plentiful
seeds
of cucumber
& squash
lettuce
& peas
to plant;
warm sun
on my
cheek,
is to miss

the anxiety
of loss —
its icy
silver
claw —
almost
entirely.

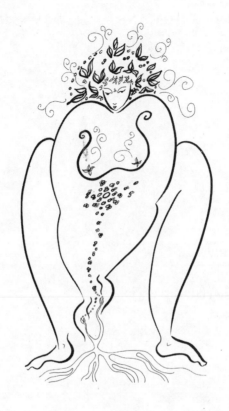

It takes so little to make me happy:
An hour of planting
cucumbers
squash
tomatoes
is an hour filled with gold.

LOVING HUMANS

For Aung San Suu Kyi

Loving humans
is tricky
sometimes
a slap
in the face
is all you get
for doing it
just right.

Loving humans is a job
like any other
only
more
bumps
on the way
to work
which is full on
all the time.

Loving humans
makes us
want
to invite
ourselves to tea

with rancid
dictators
we think we
can convince
of our
story's side
while all
they think
about
while
we sit & dream
is how
they can
get away
with
poisoning
our tea

and how
if only they
had
enough tea
already
brewed
they could
waterboard us
to death
with it.

Loving humans
means
writing poems & songs
novels & plays, slogans, chants
& protest signs
our critics
want
to stone
us for
while
we think of
them
as people
under different
circumstances
we might
be able
to help.

There is
indeed
a Buddha
in
every one
of us.
Loving humans
with all
our clear &

unmistakable
reluctance
to evolve
makes this hard
for most humans
to see.

But not you.

DYING

For those who with our taxes die of torture

What is it like
dying?

Is it like
sinking
into a bath
of warm
milk?

Is it like
lying naked
in the
sun
those first
truly
warm
days of
spring
after
a winter
that
froze
your teeth?

Dying
I think
can be
like that.

Above all,
it is yours:
it is
a safe
place.

They may
be
electrocuting
your
toes
at
the time
or
pulling out
your
fingernails
or causing
your
terrified
heart
to stop

in other
ingenious
ways.

But dying
you
escape
them
into peace.

They will
never
know
something
only
you
can have:

Dying is yours
alone,
precious
human being
whatever
you have done.

Dying is
your secret.

LOVING OUR LEADERS

For Beverly

I find I am loving
our leaders
unconditionally
as I know
I am
loved
myself.

I love him
I love her
I love the girls
the grandmother
the friends
& deceased
grandparents
& ancestors:
I especially
love
the
dog. And would hope
for him
soon
a cat.

They
are us
you know,
our leaders;

finally
leading
ourselves
as us:

Who we really
are:

More perfect
for
our imperfections:

Unconditionally
& forever
loved

human beings.

I GAVE IT FREELY

I gave
it
freely
this life
that
pours
through
me
abundant.

Why was
it not
the
same
with
you?

And then
I saw:

You
are a
consumer
of

life
&
inside
you
it lies
trapped.

It is
never
permitted
to
continue
its
journey:
You
hoard
it
as if
there really
is
no
tomorrow.

Life
entering you
never
passes
to
another.

Life
having
entered
you
looks
out
of your
eyes
at me:
Get me
out!
it
begs.

But I
do not
know
how.

ENCOUNTERING

Encountering
you
I
struck
a
wall:
You
do not
even
seem
to know
that
you
are hiding
behind
it.

These are
not
poems —
unsent
messages
to
the
deaf.

MIND SHINE

For Michelle

Woman
of color
lighting up
the
dark.

A FEW MONKS

Having lived
as a monk
myself: I recognize us.

Those long decades
of soundless
trekking through
the squealing
forests.

Those predawn
meditations
whose
insights
ramble on
for years.

The young ones
left
behind us
abject:
their well-aimed
curses
hurled

with venom
at our
departing
enlightenment-
seduced
necks.

Wake up!

The Buddhas
you set
before yourselves
polished and
carved
with their painted eyes
and carmine
lips
not to mention
their
well-kissed
feet
resemble more
and more

the women
& children
you left
behind.

Enough!

Stay home
if you
possibly
can.

A few monks
need
a
cuddle
buddy.

That warm leg
near
dawn
flung carelessly
over
an even
warmer
thigh.

The smell
of breath
not just
its movement;
a child's
trusting hug
& earthy sweat:

Carved
wood
or
stone
no matter its
well-kissed
perfection
or what beloved
teacher
it
represents

in
the midnight
hour

reminds us
mostly
of a
wound

we are not
wise
enough
to forget.

EVEN SO

Love, if it is love, never goes away.
It is embedded in us,
like seams of gold in the Earth,
waiting for light,
waiting to be struck.

ALICE LOVES ME (OR, THEY HAVE A BAD TRACK RECORD OF MASS GRAVES)

Yes
I know
they have
a bad habit
of
coming
to your door
before
dawn;
before even
your littlest
is awake
&
waiting
for
your
morning
smile;

your scent
of tobacco
&
apples.

I know
encountering
you
on
a deserted
road
they have
a tendency
to drive
their subsidized
jeeps
& armored
tanks
into
your defenseless
body;
loaded
down
with
firewood,
water
in leaking
plastic
jugs,
old clothes
from the
missionary
dump,

&
your
broken
heart;

pushing you
to slow
surrender
of
all you
were
&
are.

They have
a bad
track
record
of
mass graves.

Looking at
the calm-
appearing
Spanish countryside
of
actual
Spain
one Sunday

driving
to see
Granada,
Seville,
Córdoba,
the Alhambra
& traces
of our
Moorish
roots
the driver said:
over there
& there
& there
& there
all mass graves
&
maybe Lorca*
in
one of them.

This
terror
is not
new.

---

* Federico García Lorca, extraordinary Spanish poet and
playwright assassinated by fascists near his home in Spain
in 1936.

What is new
is that
on the ether
now
I can
tell you:
I know
what is
happening
to you.

Wherever
it is
happening
whoever
is doing
it.

I want you
to know
that
& so
when you are
facing
your
final
eternal
moment

of
transformation;
whether by heat
or cold
uzi
or
machete
or "simple"
or complicated
by death
rape
or scorn;
your tears
causing
much amusement;
your efforts
to hide
your
shame
hilarious
to men
& boys
circling
your pain;

Remember
this —
say it

& know
it
is true:

Alice loves me
Alice *loves* me

and I am not blamed for this.

She knows —
& is weeping
even
in her sleep
while they laugh —

she knows
& keeps
the record
that
this
unspeakable
violation

of all of us
so briefly human

is happening
to me.

MORNING

For Kaleo

&
so
we
lie
entwined
sun
on
our
eyes

knowing
our
heaven

&
sleeping
the
cat
between
us.

INDEX OF POEMS

ABOUT THE AUTHOR

© Vaschelle André, Divine Photography

*T*o sit in peace, free, with a collard green leaf on my head! To know that all I thought as a child is true: that cats dream and are natural queens and kings; that dogs know us through and through. That monkeys are everything. That Earth is alive for all to recognize, finally. It has been and is, a good life, and I am satisfied, grateful, enchanted by it. There is no future or past, only this moment from which to grow and to feel the eternal sunshine, rain, and wind on my petals, leaves, and stem.

Such is this mystery.

In 2009 I was awarded the James Weldon Johnson Medal for Literature. I've received other prizes and awards, but I like mentioning this one because James Weldon Johnson wrote the "Negro National Anthem" ("Lift Every Voice and Sing"), the first song I learned to sing as a child and to play on piano as a sixty-five-year-old. You can find my biography, with titles of my work, on my website:

 www.alicewalkersgarden.com

A percentage of profits will be shared with the Margaret Okari Children's Foundation.

www.okarichildren.com

The Margaret Okari Children's Foundation is dedicated to helping AIDS orphans in Africa. We are committed to building the physical, spiritual, and educational foundation of the children of the Kisii region in Kenya, whose parents have died of AIDS, by engaging remaining family members, the greater community of Kisii, and interested stakeholders in assisting these children in realizing their full potential.

ABOUT THE ILLUSTRATOR

Shiloh McCloud is a visionary artist and teacher who has worked in the creativity movement for over sixteen years. Her work is dedicated to positive media and providing images and teachings that inspire healing and transformation. Shiloh is the author of five creativity journals and is currently working on a novel. She owns a gallery and founded Cosmic Cowgirls University, which offers courses online and on campus in Sonoma County, California. Shiloh is also the founder of Palm of Her Hand, a foundation that collaborates with visionaries on projects that bring positive media to the world.

 www.shilohsophia.com

PALM OF HER HAND FOUNDATION

The mission of Palm of Her Hand is to bring awareness to the importance and healing power of creative self-expression in the lives of every person on the planet. We collaborate with artists, poets, and dreamers to bring visionary education, publish transformational books, and produce inspirational art events.

 www.palmofherhand.com

NEW WORLD LIBRARY is dedicated to publishing books and other media that inspire and challenge us to improve the quality of our lives and the world.

We are a socially and environmentally aware company, and we strive to embody the ideals presented in our publications. We recognize that we have an ethical responsibility to our customers, our staff members, and our planet.

We serve our customers by creating the finest publications possible on personal growth, creativity, spirituality, wellness, and other areas of emerging importance. We serve New World Library employees with generous benefits, significant profit sharing, and constant encouragement to pursue their most expansive dreams.

As a member of the Green Press Initiative, we print an increasing number of books with soy-based ink on 100 percent postconsumer-waste recycled paper. Also, we power our offices with solar energy and contribute to nonprofit organizations working to make the world a better place for us all.

Our products are available
in bookstores everywhere.
For our catalog, please contact:

New World Library
14 Pamaron Way
Novato, California 94949

Phone: 415-884-2100 or 800-972-6657
Catalog requests: Ext. 50
Orders: Ext. 52
Fax: 415-884-2199
Email: escort@newworldlibrary.com

To subscribe to our electronic newsletter, visit
www.newworldlibrary.com

HELPING TO PRESERVE OUR ENVIRONMENT

3,147
trees were saved

New World Library uses 100% postconsumer-waste recycled paper for our books whenever possible, even if it costs more. During 2011 this choice saved the following precious resources:

ENERGY	WASTEWATER	GREENHOUSE GASES	SOLID WASTE
22 MILLION BTU	600,000 GAL.	770,000 LB.	225,000 LB.

Environmental impact estimates were made using the Environmental Defense Fund Paper Calculator @ www.papercalculator.org.